THE PRAYING ATHLETE™

PHOTOGRAPHY

QUOTE BOOK - VOL 3

Robert B. Walker

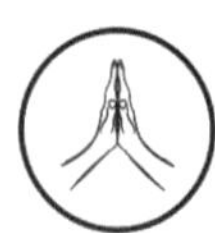

The Praying Athlete Photography Quote Book Volume 3

Published by The Core Media Group, Inc., P.O. Box 2037, Indian Trail, NC 28079.

Quotes written by Robert B. Walker. Photography by Robert B. Walker & Ashlyn Helms.
Cover and Interior design by Ashlyn Helms.

Printed in the United States of America.

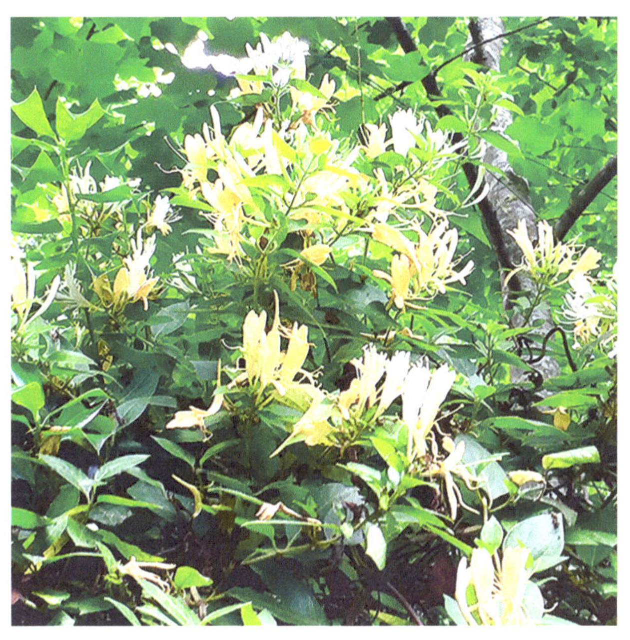

"And continue to walk surrendered to the extravagant love of Christ, for he surrendered his life as a sacrifice for us. His great love for us was pleasing to God, like an aroma of adoration—a sweet healing fragrance."
Ephesians 5:2 TPT

"Love the game and understand it is a privilege and honor to play. This will engage the reason you play and give you rewards and blessings from the game."

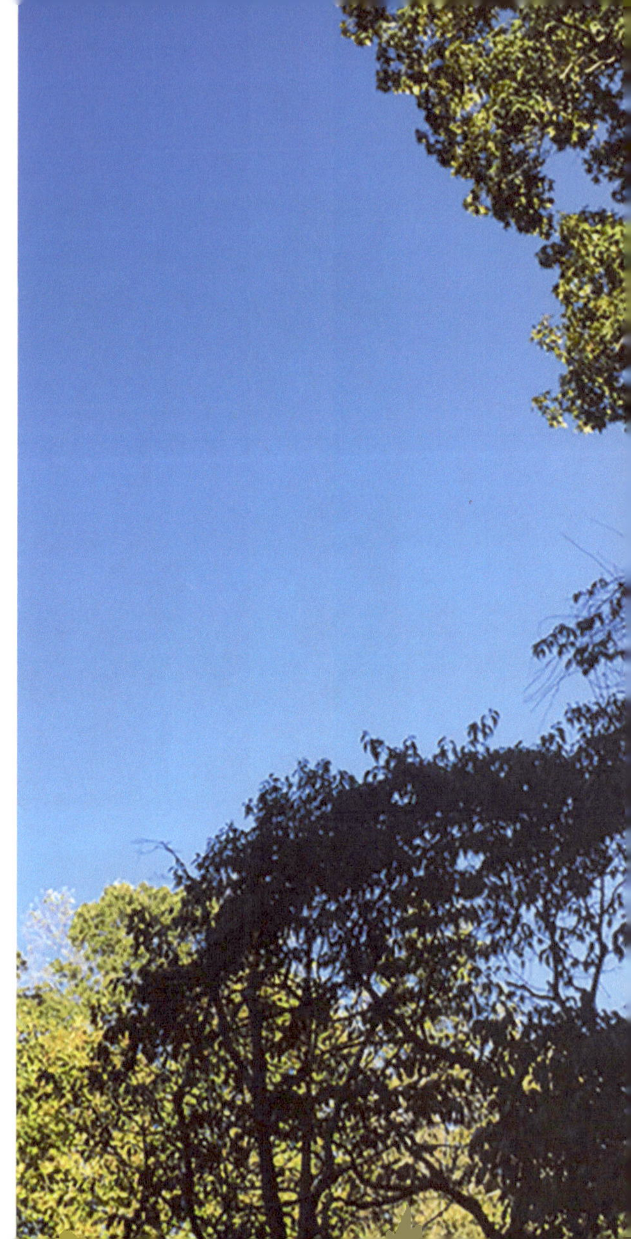

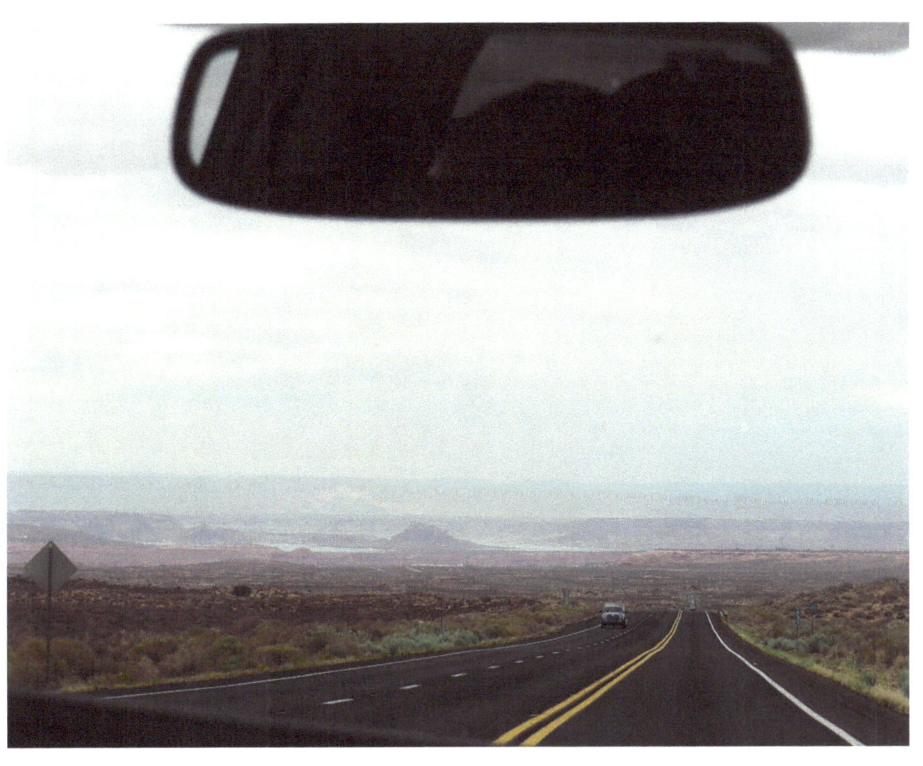

"God allows detours to occur in our life to find the more He has in store for us. Trust him!"

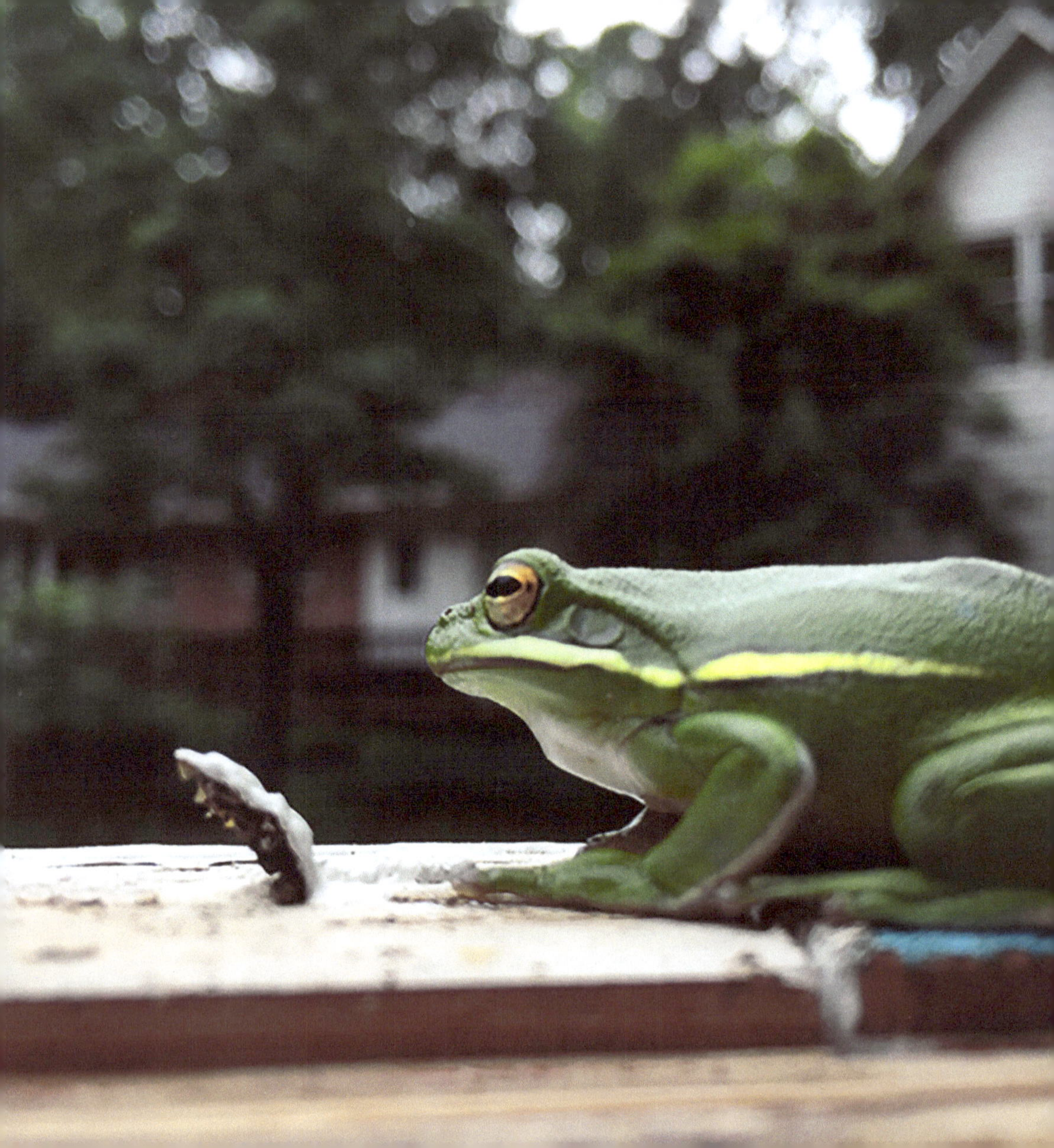

"Sometimes you have to stop jumping around, pause, and take it all in."

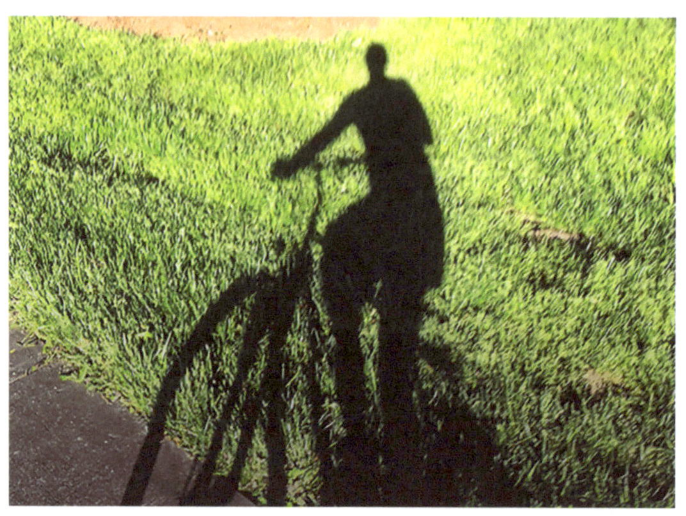

"Many times, we can be fooled by the images of life. We begin to think that we are bigger and better than others. Let us not be fooled by the images, but be inspired by the potential within us."

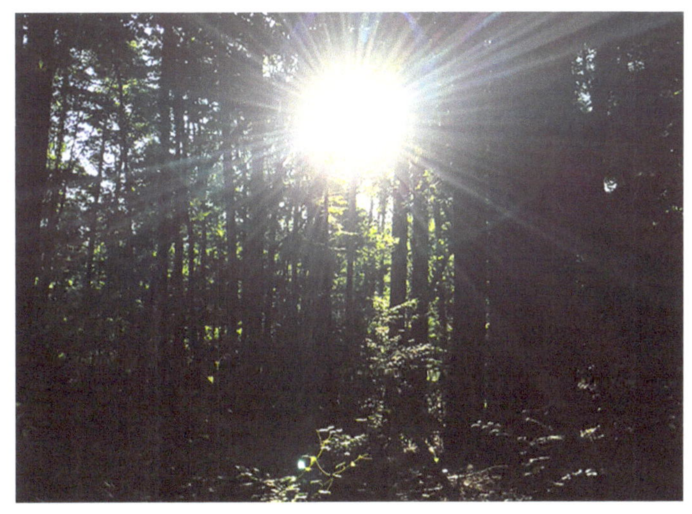

"How you respond to conflict exposes your character."

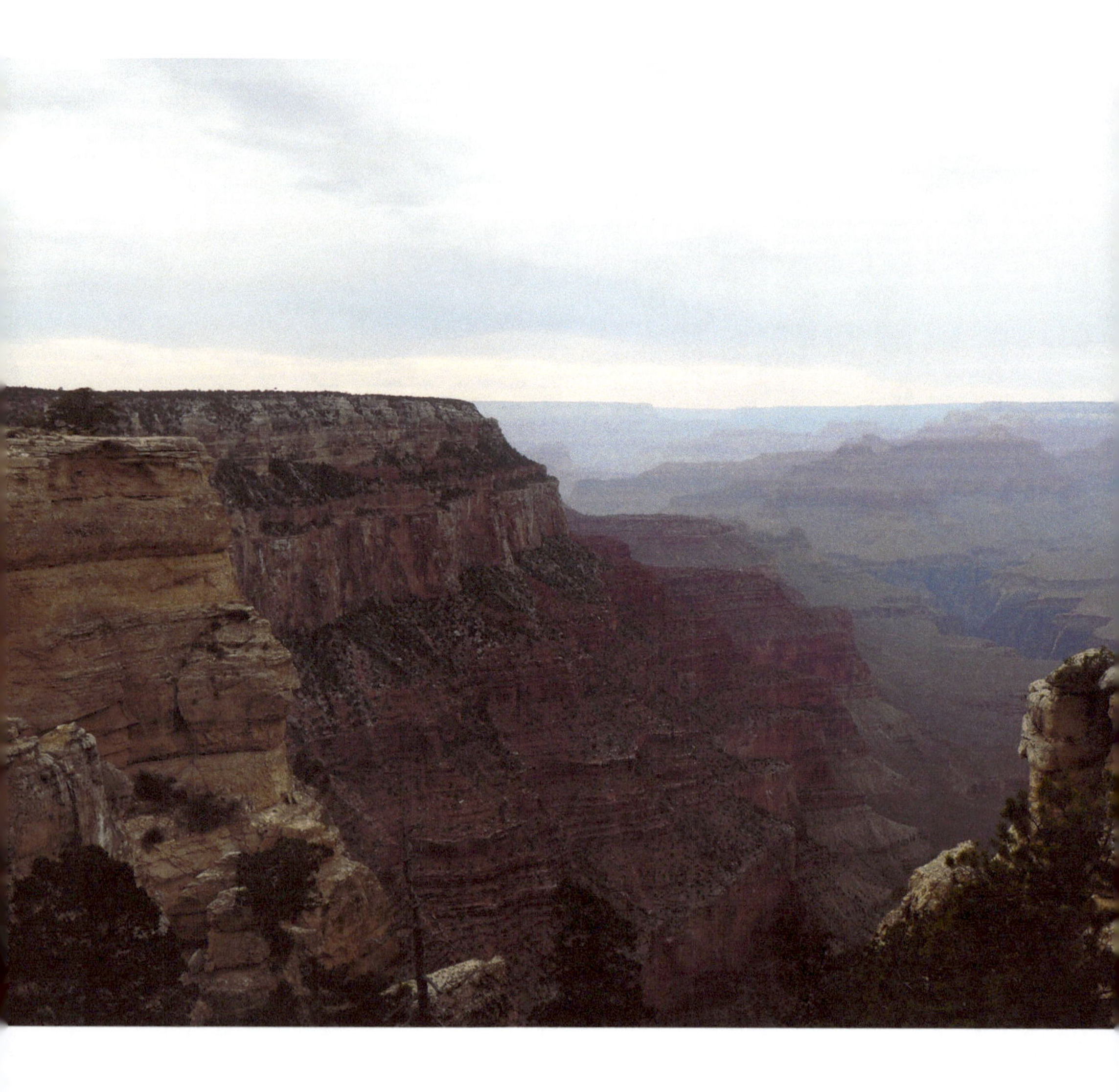

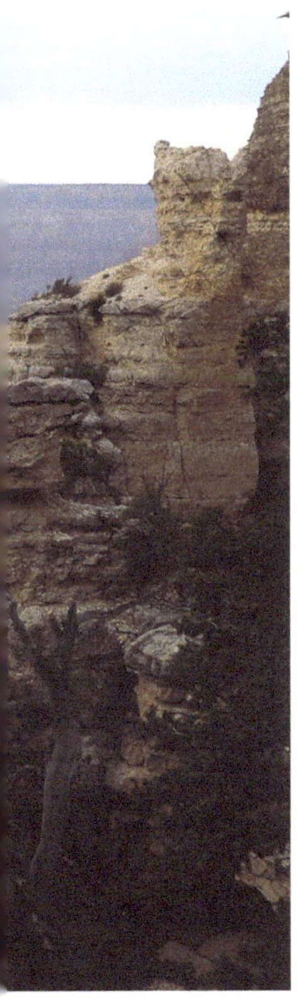

"The daily grind of climbing every mountain, getting over every hurdle, and pushing yourself when you feel like you cannot make it another day is all part of the chase. We must challenge ourselves to carry on, despite being deterred and detoured along the journey. The dream is alive deep within your soul. You can make that dream reality by pushing yourself daily to fight every battle and chase that dream. Our past losses become our permanent gains with the wisdom gained from our journey of yesterday."

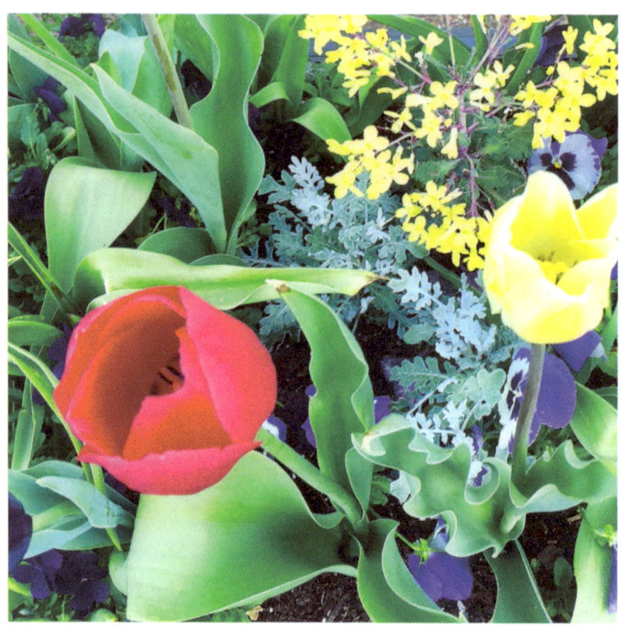

"Everyday make it a point to standout and bloom a little brighter where you are planted. People will see the smile on your face and the joy in your lifestyle, then they will seek your joy!"

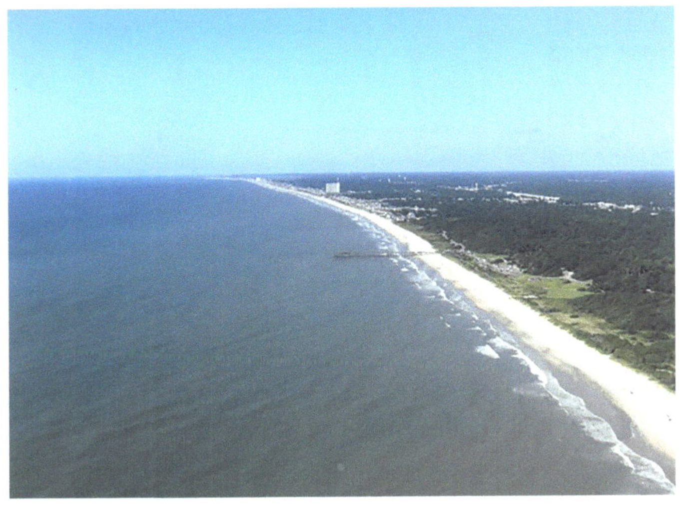

"You will accomplish so much in the life you have ahead. But, the true key to a successful life is what you will do today—to be better, to do better, and to be the best you in the life ahead. It is today that matters most."

"When you say you are tired and you say you are not sure how much more you can go, stop, pause and view this photo of a couple working out. Both of them are on walkers and still giving it their all. What about you? They inspired me when I saw them at the YMCA while I was working out. What thoughts come to your mind?"

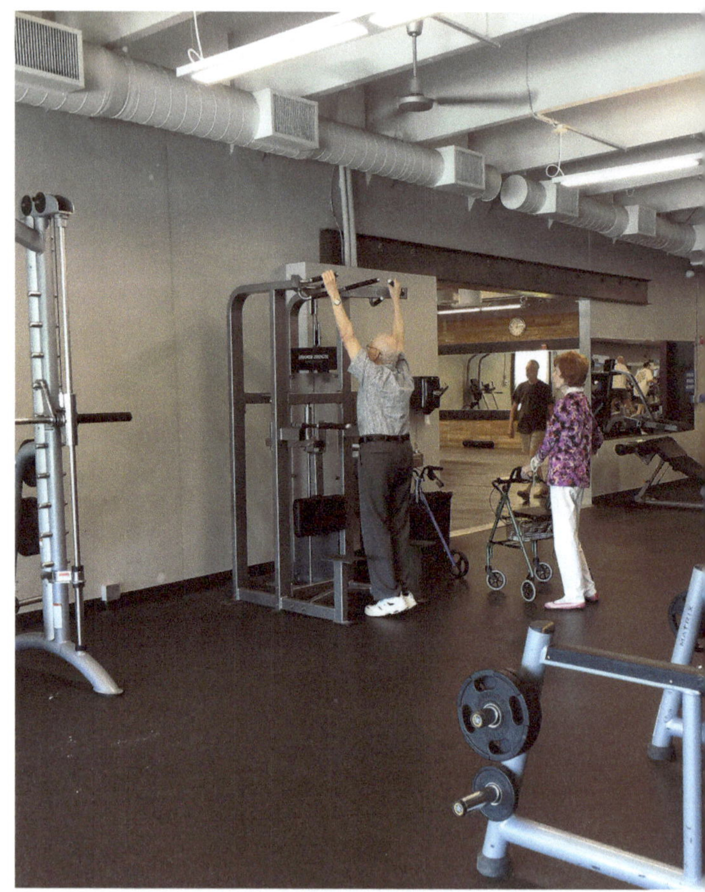

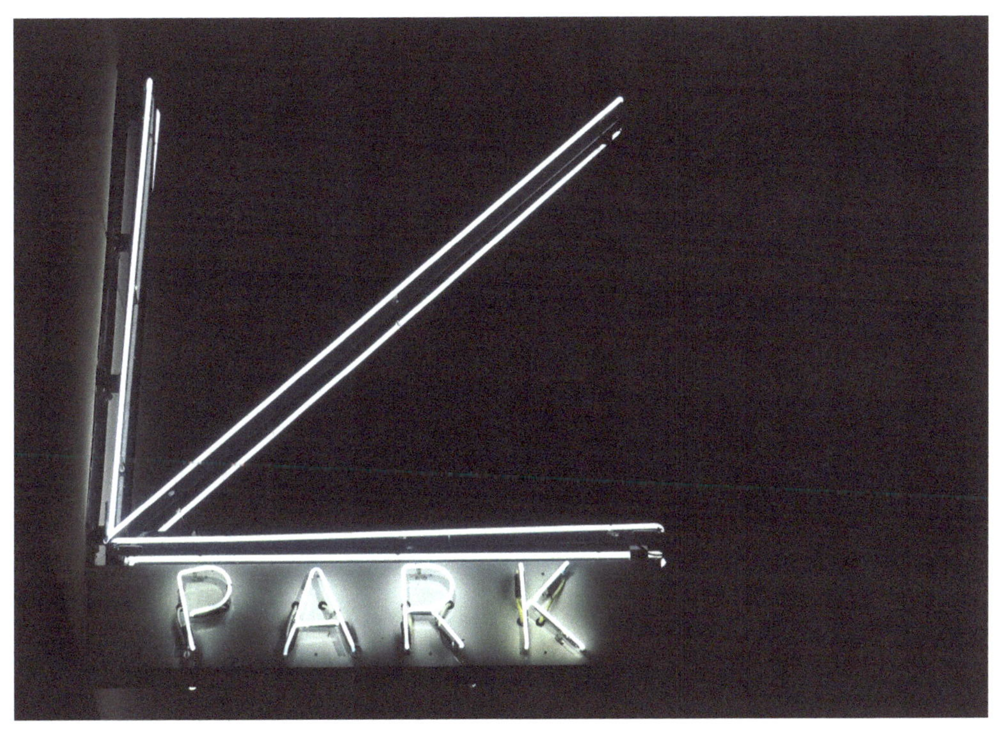

"The reason successful people fail is because of their gradual inability to say no to their own desires and wants that can trip them up. Practice daily saying no to whatever is distracting you from achieving your personal success."

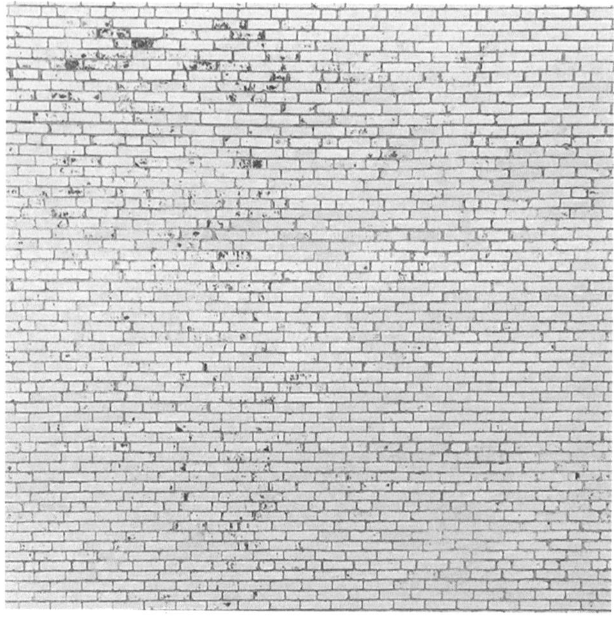

"In this life, people will discount you because of where you live, the car you drive, your appearance, your job, your race, or your family. Remind yourself that this life is temporary. Therefore, focus on Heaven, where you will never be judged or discounted for any reason. His perfection awaits."

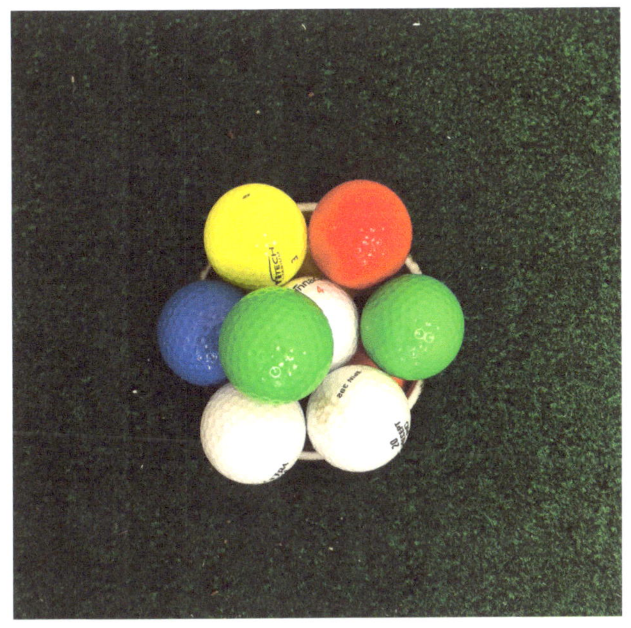

"What does this picture say to you? To me it says, if you practice and practice and practice you will achieve great things. The fun is in the practice to see how great you can be. Practice builds confidence."

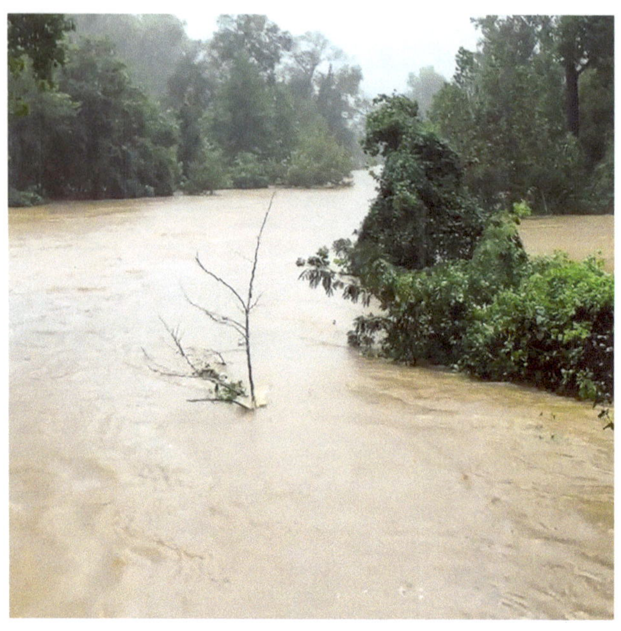

"Sometimes our lives feel out of control and everything seems to be crashing in all at the same time. But, know the waters will recede and the storm will pass. The sun will shine on you again and your new day will begin. Never give up on what you believe in your heart."

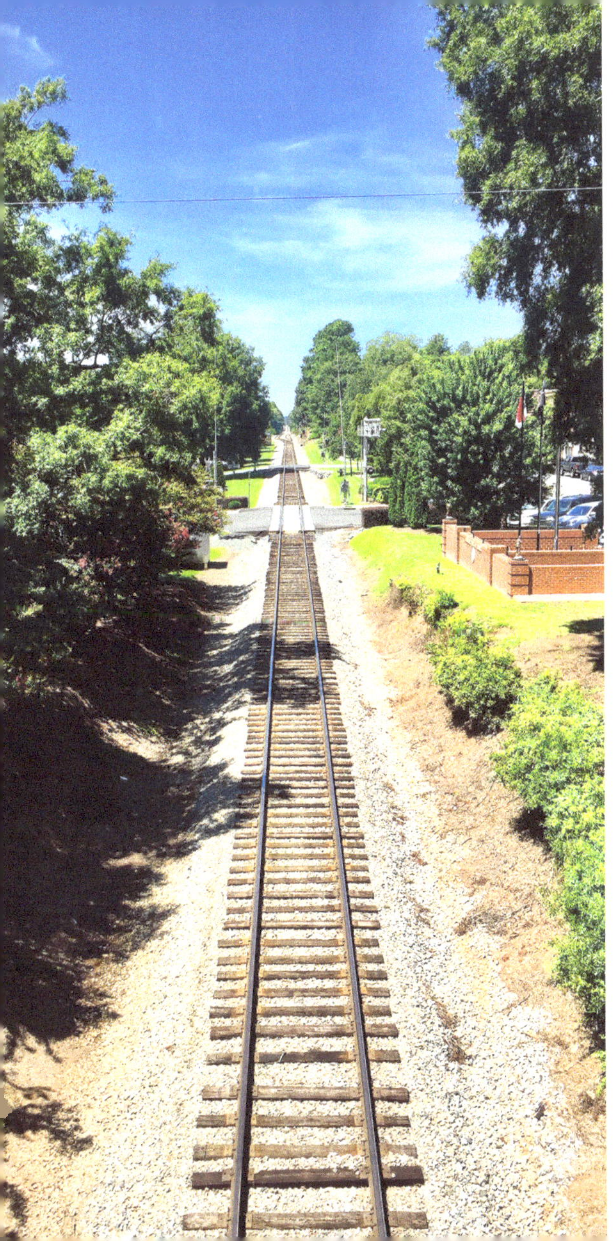

"Look closely and you will see the cross in this picture. At first glance, after taking this photo. I did not notice the cross. But then this thought came to me: The cross will carry you much further than you ever imagined. Stay true to God and He will take you on an endless path of success. It will be bumpy and rough along the tracks of life. The way to true success is to keep going one track at a time, and stay on the straight and narrow path. Others will try and persuade you to get off the track, but as you can see, the journey is long. You do not have time to be distracted from the goals that are within your spirit. Do not allow negative thoughts or words of discouragement to push you off the tracks of life. Be reminded that He has placed you on this track."

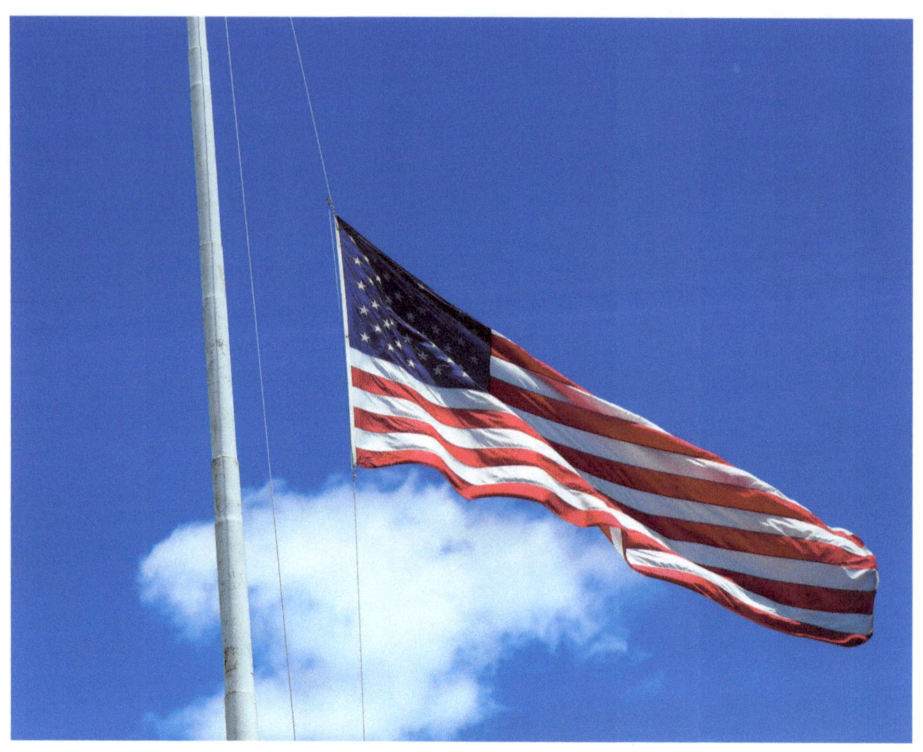

"What you honor and serve will move into your life. What you do not honor and serve will eventually move out of your life. Take time to honor and serve those you want to have a priority in your life. This grace, service, acceptance and honor will bring peace, love, harmony and hugs of affirmation."

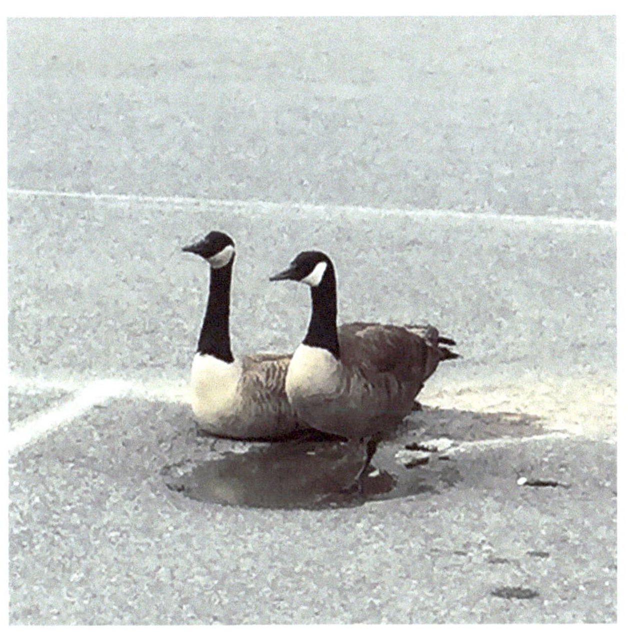

"It does not matter the size of your success,
but the contentment found where you are."

"Shut the door on the negative voices. Be creative in your work! Be outstanding in your effort! Make your performance standout like nothing anyone has ever seen!"

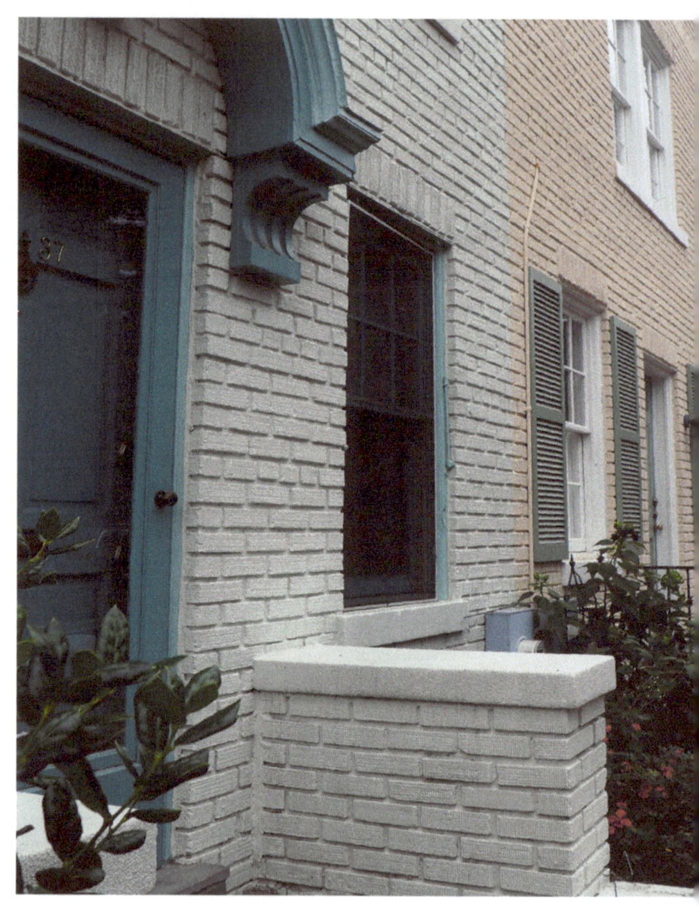

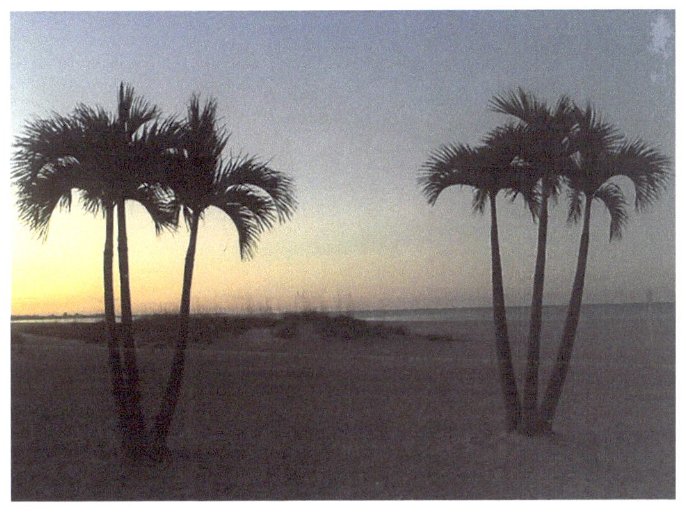

"For where two or three gather in My name, there am I with them."
Matthew 18:20

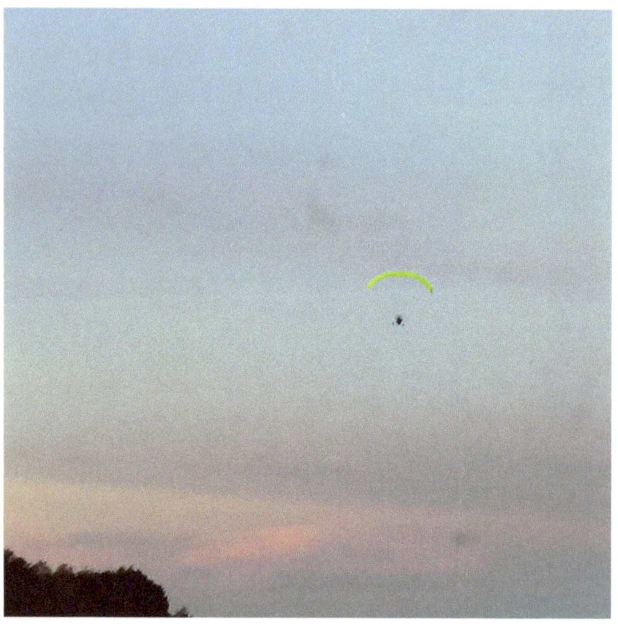

"Know this and believe it, you must strip the negativity on your life's journey and capture the joy that is now in your reach. You must press and strive to keep the drive alive deep within your soul. As you embrace your journey, what is ahead is unexplainable. You will one day soon find yourself shaking with excitement and awe as God reveals and delivers your heart's desires. Stay true to you!"

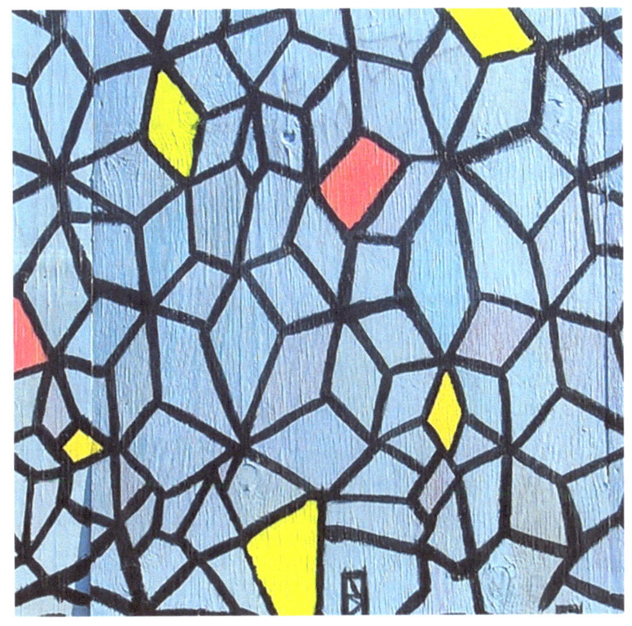

"What is one way to build a great reputation as an outstanding player that plays with heart? REPETITION. Doing the right thing over and over again. Doing it well with passion and energy. Perfecting the reps even when no else is looking. While taking reps you are always reminded it will impact your reputation. Whether in practice or life you will find yourself with great reputation that will precede you when each repetition has value to you."

"Standing on a pedestal will only be temporary; it can easily be kicked out from under you. Instead, build a platform built on a strong foundation of faith, hope and love."

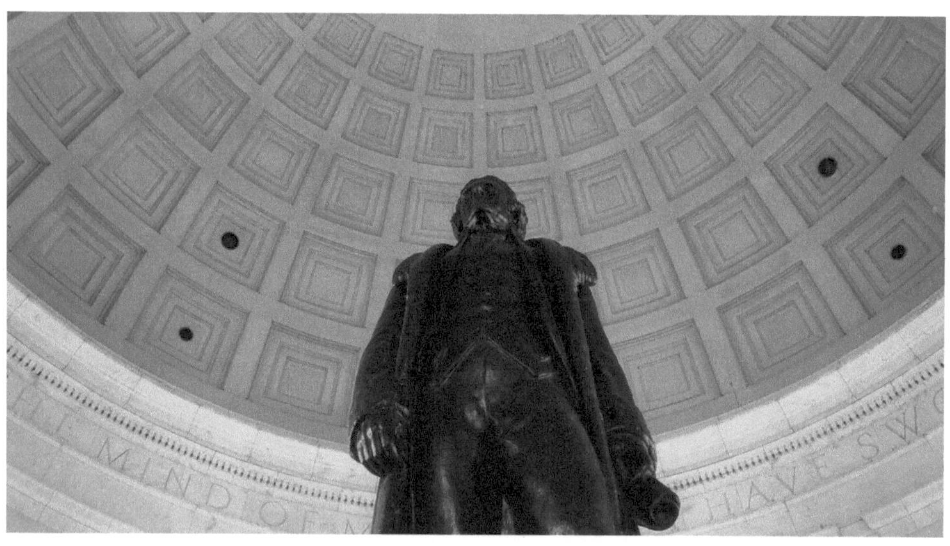

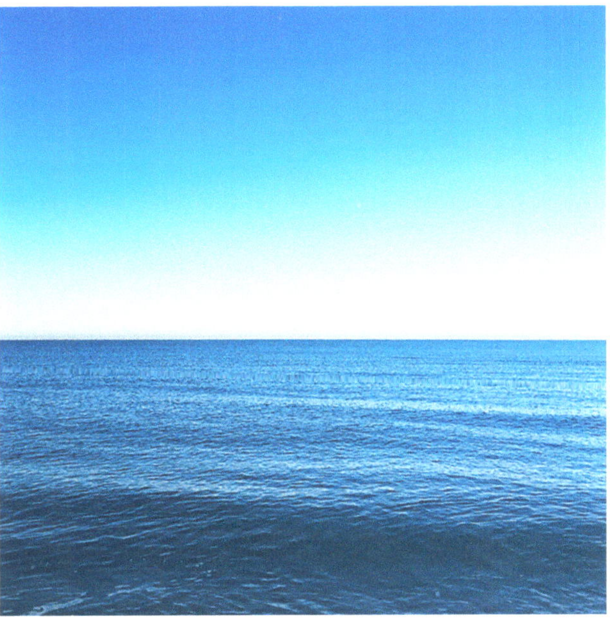

"Your eyes cannot see the endless blessings God has planned for you!"

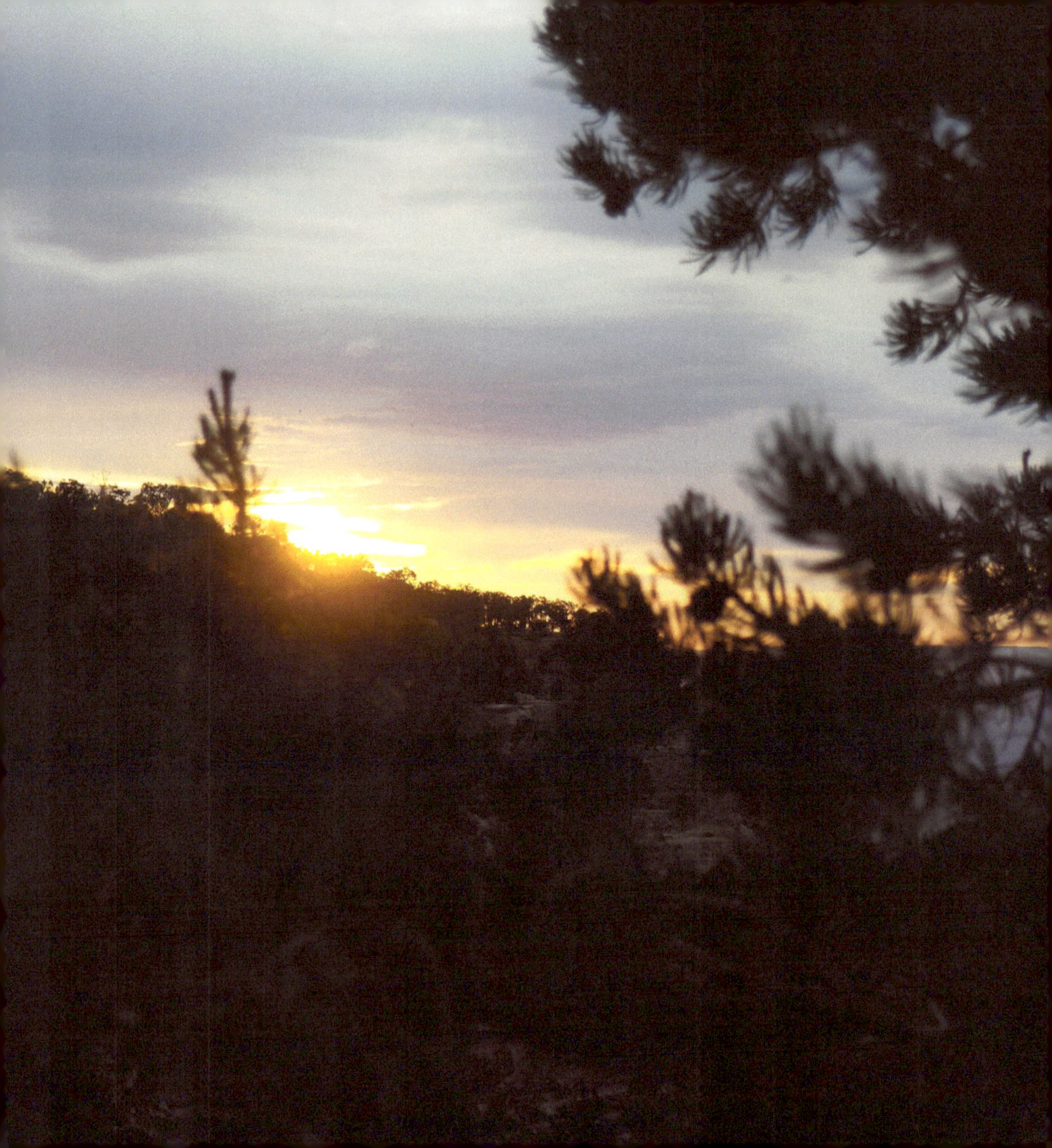

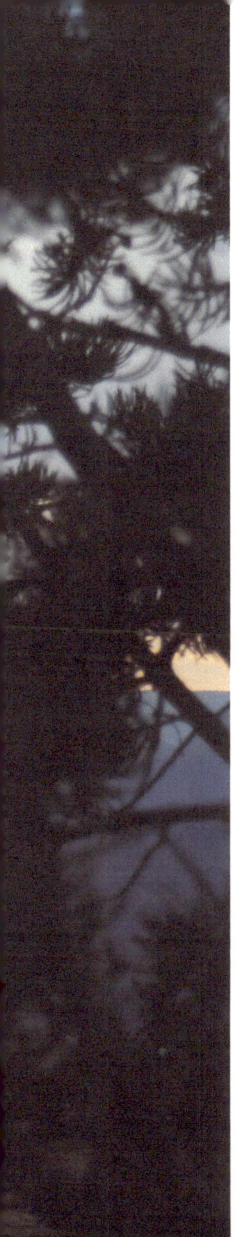

"When you arrive—no matter the way—it is what you do to prove you belong with your daily performance to project the wow on those that see you."

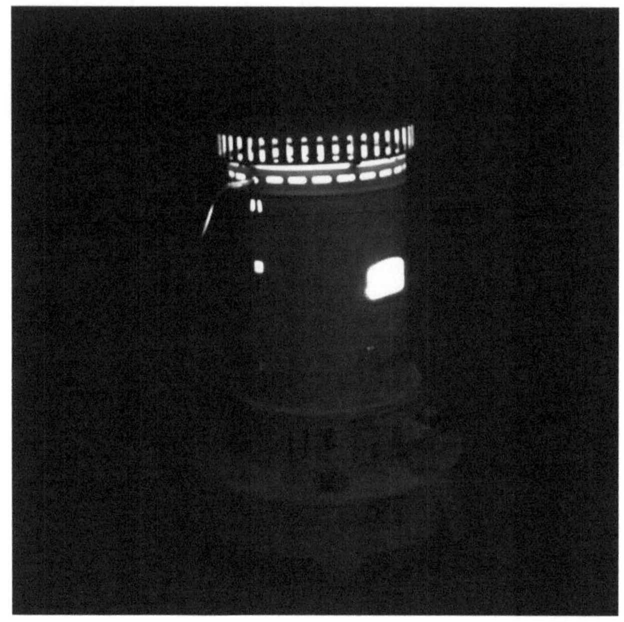

"Remember you are significant and nothing about you or your talent is insignificant. You will need whatever seems insignificant at some point. Be prepared and stay ready to light the fuse that powers your soul to the greatness within!"

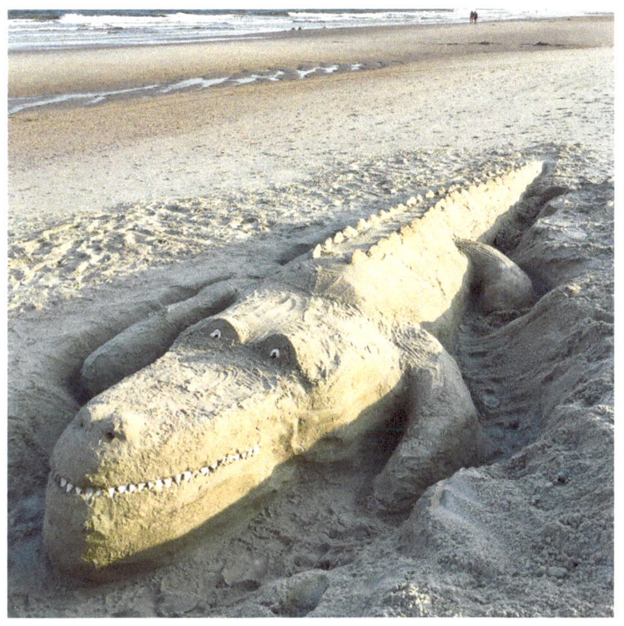

"There are always good days at my main office and good days at my southern office. Both are work, just different kinds of work. Find your play in your work no matter the location."

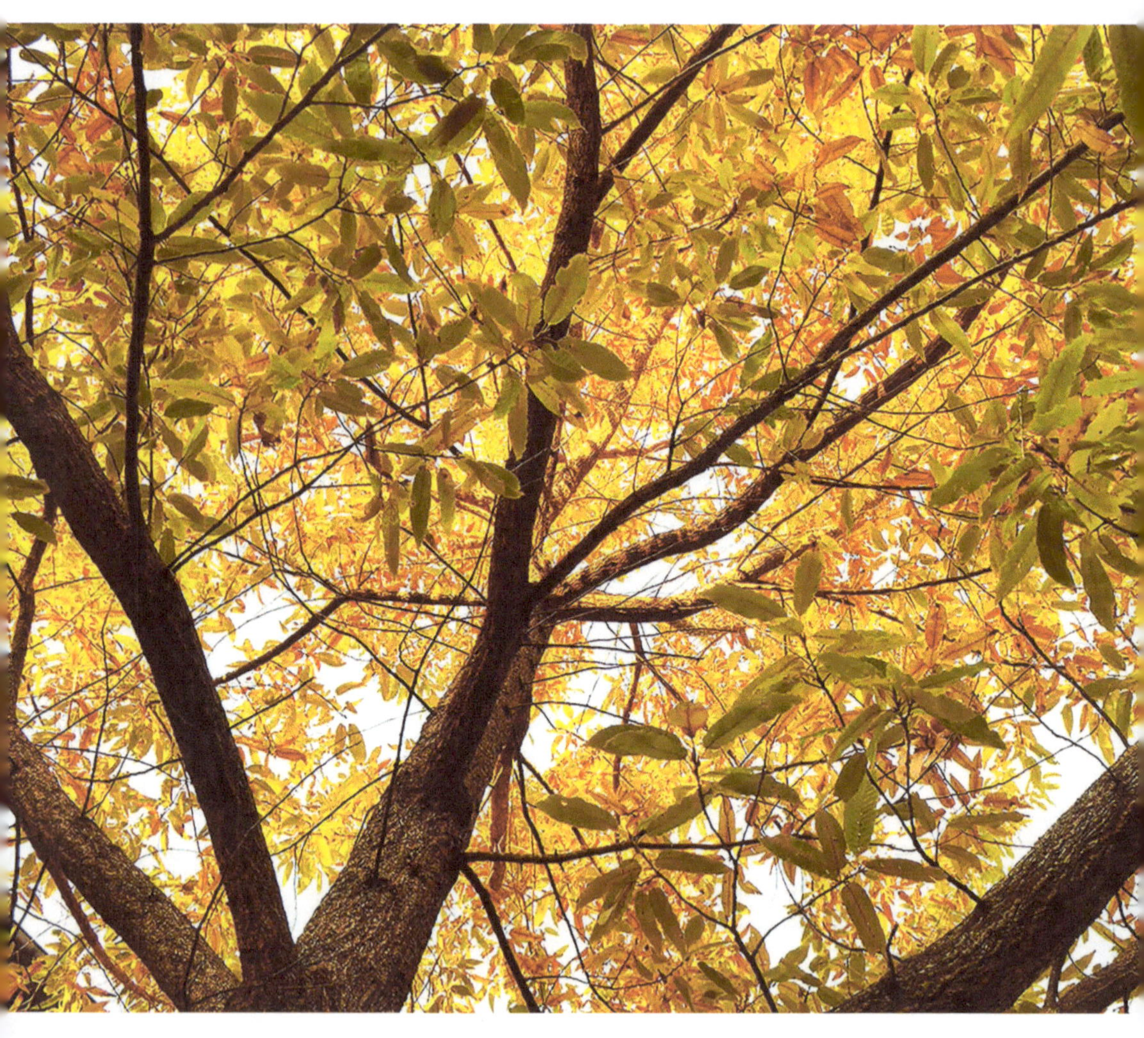

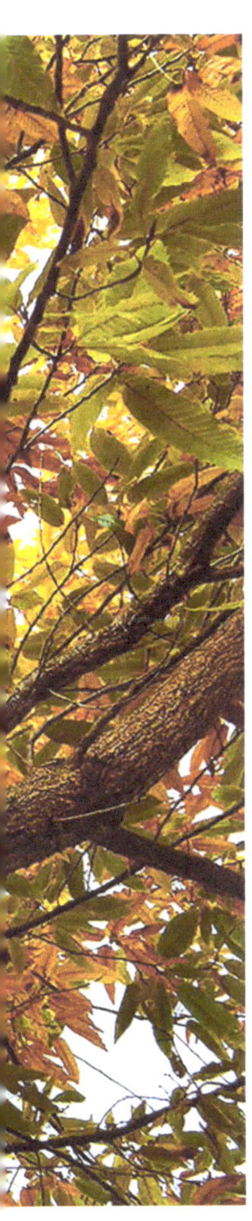

"Take a minute and look at the tree limbs. They have been reaching for the sun for many years. The tree limbs know where their growth comes from. May we strive to reach for the Son and find the power when He shines and activates our growth."

"Someone asked me how I define greatness. To me, greatness is not sacrifice, dedication, desire, commitment, confidence or any of the other cliché terms. To me, it is one word, belief. Believing is how I define greatness. Everything else flows from belief. Sometimes it can be what is between our ears that keeps us from greatness for the lack of belief. Believe and you will conceive. Then, you will birth the greatness that is from within."

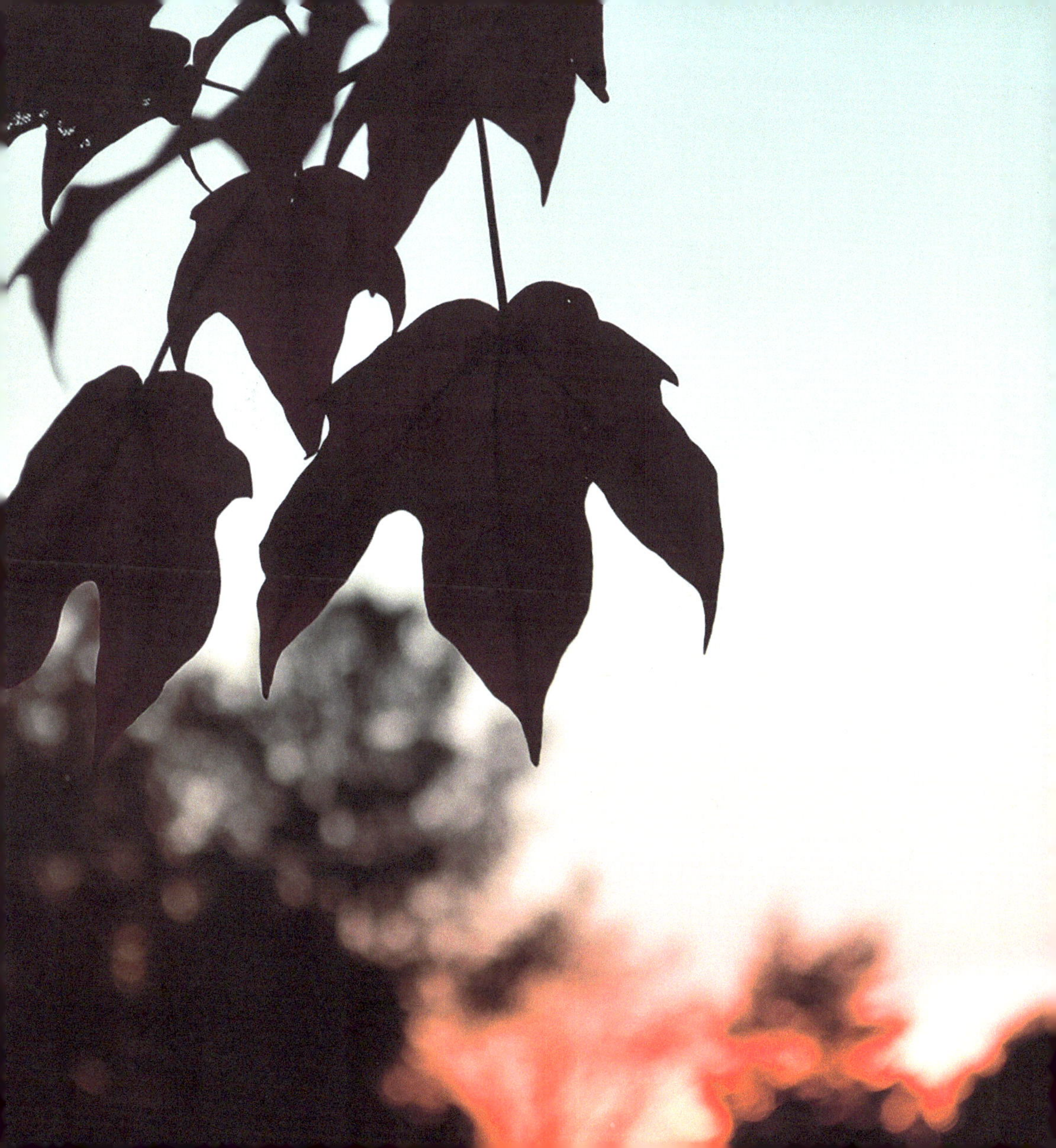

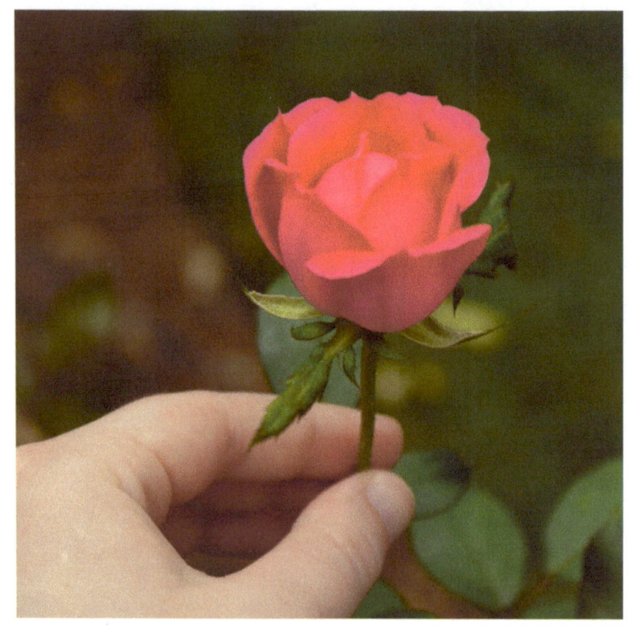

"Holding on to the fear and hurts of yesterday will paralyze your today and tomorrow."

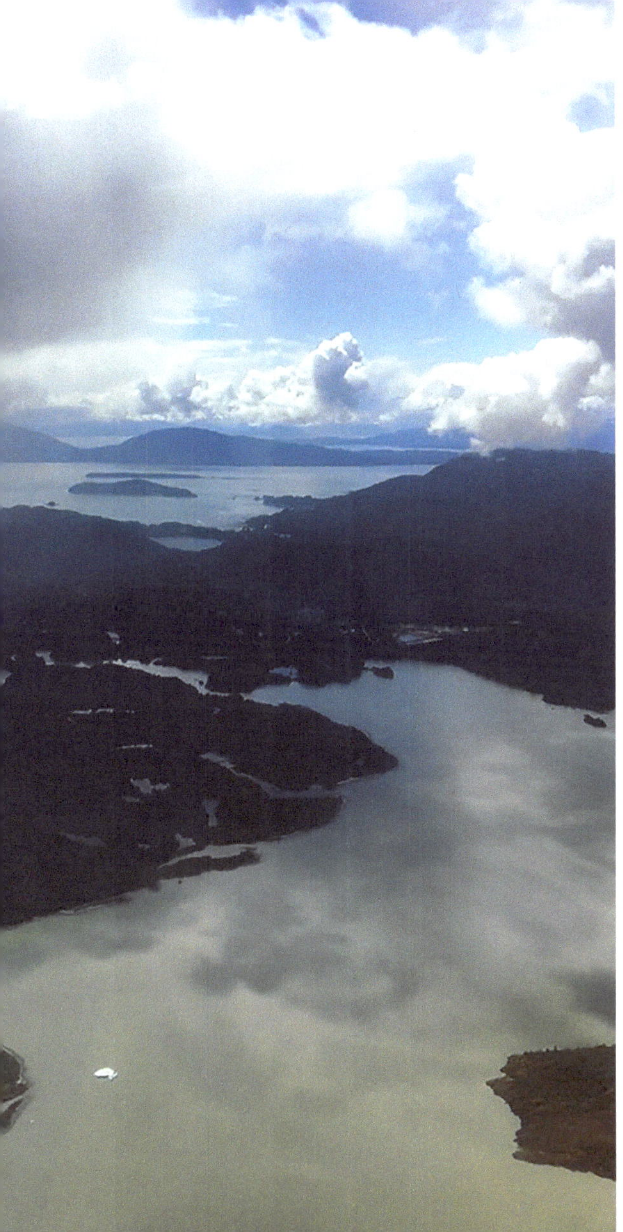

"God grants opportunities:
We must have the faith,
fearlessness, fortitude,
strength, courage and
belief to take the first step
into the unknown sea
of life. The first step will
activate your faith, then
the unknown will become
known and you will make
it to the other side. Ready!
Set! Go!."

"Today did not come by chance. It came only by using the gifts you were blessed to receive upon your creation. Today did not come by accident; you have nourished your gifts with dedication, hard work, focus, energy, sacrifices, desire, and endurance. Therefore, play with zeal and confidence because this is your day. Nothing has changed since you started this journey on the field; the smell and the texture of the turf is the same. As you prepare today, allow yourself to gain the focus and confidence between the lines for there lies your gift of preparation and your sanctuary of peace, hope, faith and love."

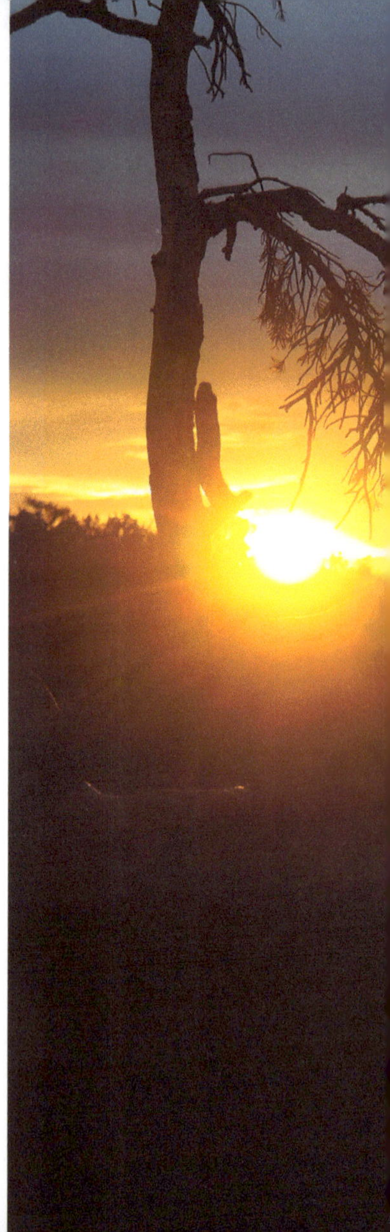

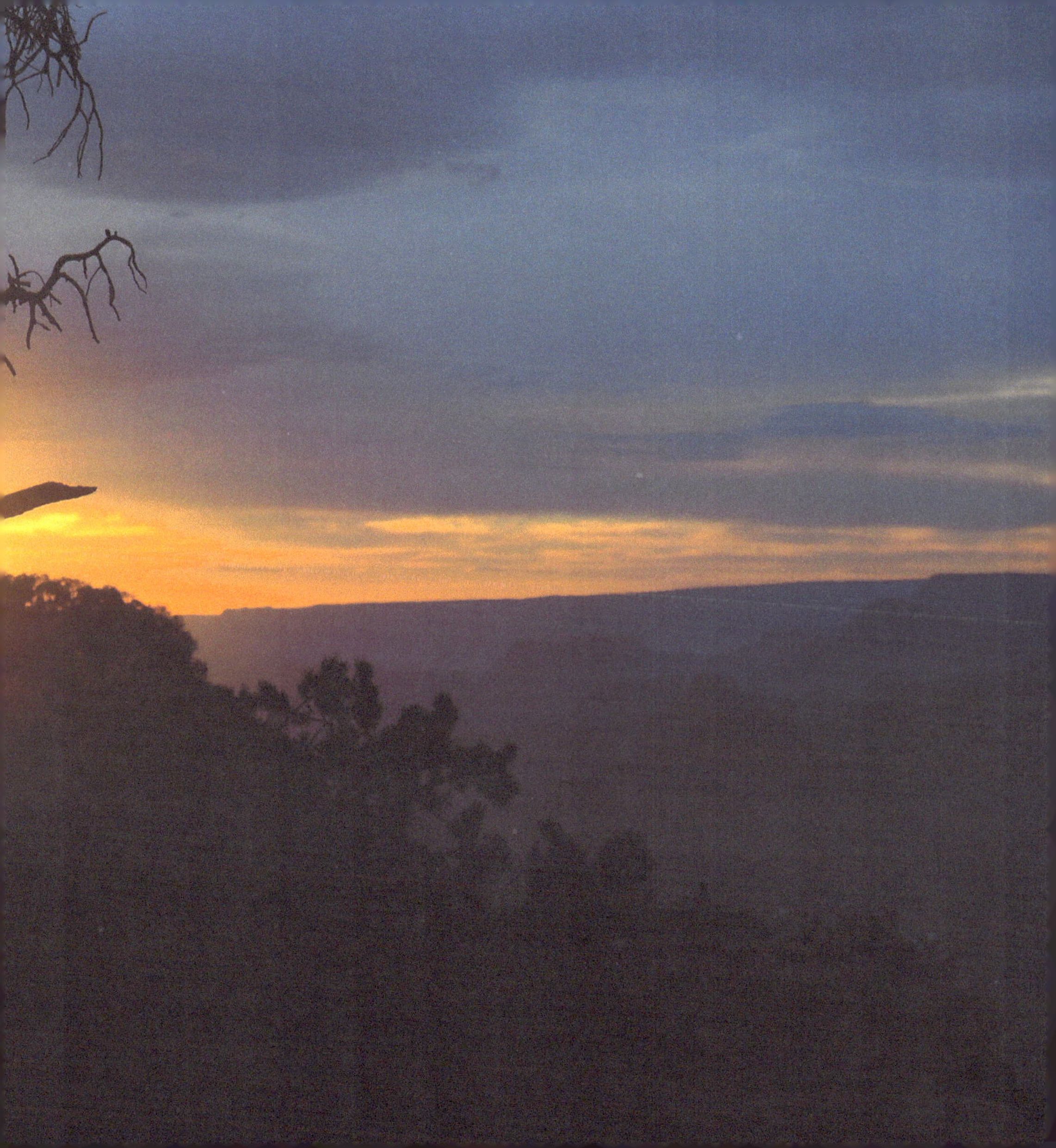

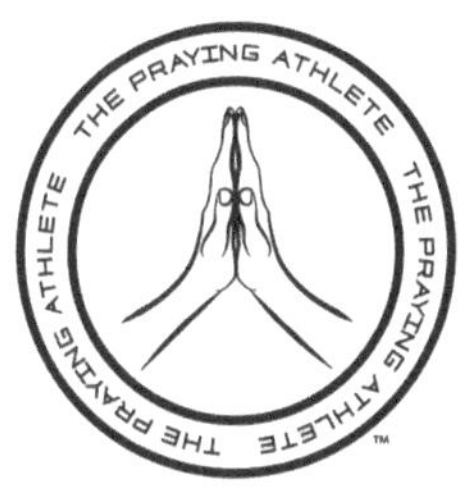

ABOUT
TPA

The Praying Athlete is a movement that creates an organic culture of prayer through an uplifting community and authentic conversation.

For more information, visit our website **www.theprayingathlete.com**.

Follow us on social media.

 **@ThePrayingAthlete**

 **@Praying_Athlete**

 **@ThePrayingAthlete**

CHECK OUT OUR
THE PRAYING ATHLETE™
QUOTE BOOK SERIES

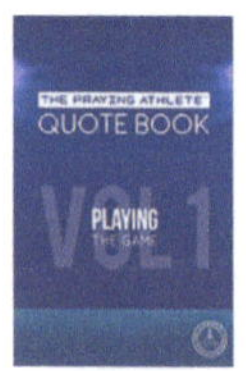

Our first volume of *The Praying Athlete Quote Book* addresses the topic of playing the game. Quotes and thoughts from Robert B. Walker, paired with Scripture from God's Word, allow readers to get a good idea about what playing a good game looks like.

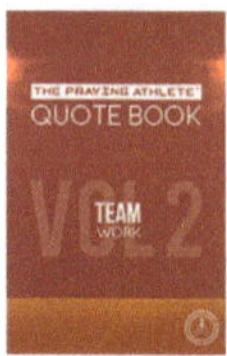

Our second volume of *The Praying Athlete Quote Book* addresses the topic of teamwork. Quotes and thoughts from Robert B. Walker, paired with Scripture from God's Word, allow readers to understand what it means to be a good teammate and surround yourself with people who lift you up.

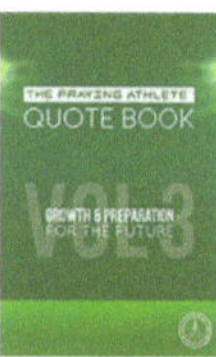

Our third volume of *The Praying Athlete Quote Book* addresses the topic of growth & preparation for the future. Quotes and thoughts from Robert B. Walker, paired with Scripture from God's Word, allow readers to know that even though the future is uncertain, there is a plan and purpose for everyone.

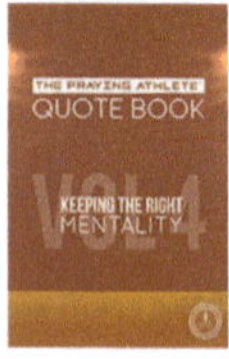

Our fourth volume of *The Praying Athlete Quote Book* addresses the topic of keeping the right mentality. Quotes and thoughts from Robert B. Walker allow readers to understand how staying in the right mindset can improve overall performance.

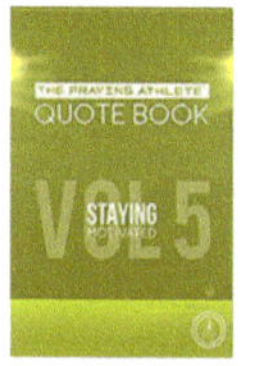

Our fifth volume of *The Praying Athlete Quote Book* addresses the topic of staying motivated. Quotes and thoughts from Robert B. Walker allow readers to become motivated to accomplish their goals, even when they feel they are not up to the task.

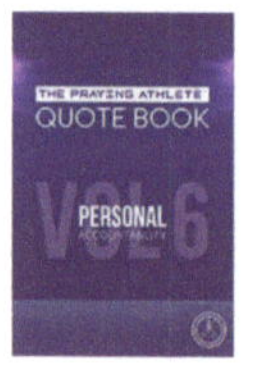

Our sixth volume of *The Praying Athlete Quote Book* addresses the topic of personal accountability. Quotes and thoughts from Robert B. Walker allow readers to think about how they can better themselves. Whether its ending a bad habit or saying no to anything that may hurt themselves or others, staying accountable will benefit one's character and performance.

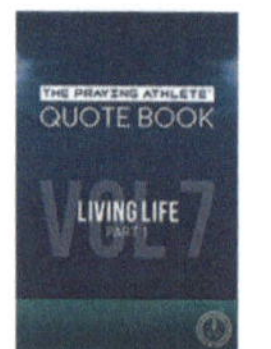

Our seventh volume of *The Praying Athlete Quote Book* addresses the topic of living life. This volume is the first part in a two part living life series. Quotes and thoughts from Robert B. Walker give readers a better understanding of how to live life to the fullest.

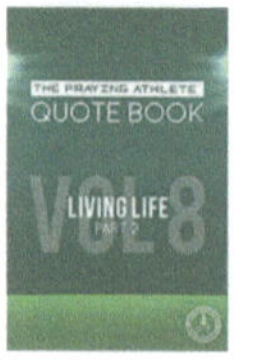

Our eighth volume of *The Praying Athlete Quote Book* addresses the topic of living life. This volume is the second part in a two part living life series. Quotes and thoughts from Robert B. Walker give readers a better understanding of how to live life to the fullest.

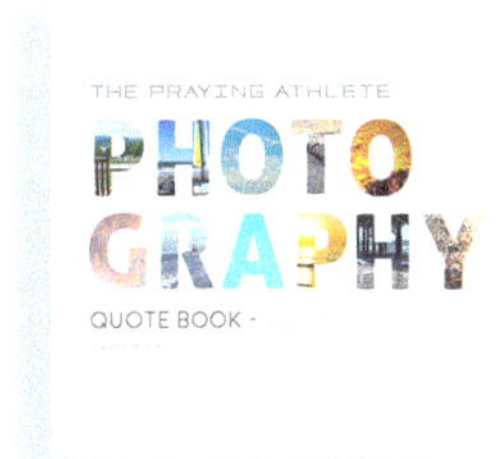

VOL. 1

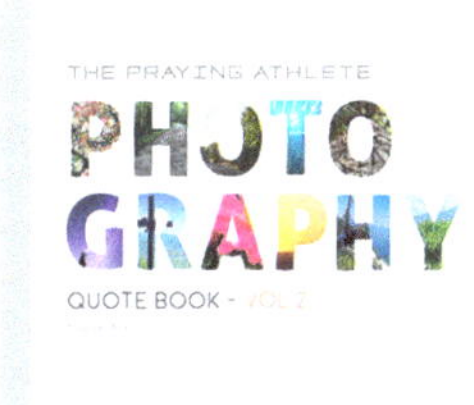

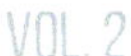

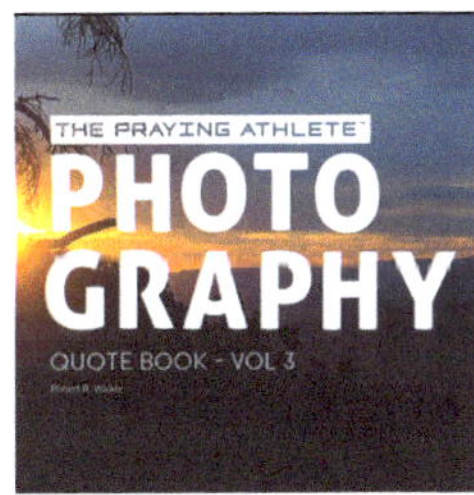

VOL. 3

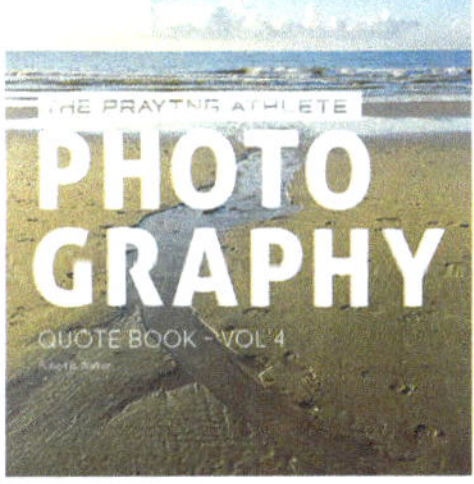

VOL. 4

The Praying Athlete Photography Quote Books celebrate God's glory and magnificence through His creation. They contain photos taken by Robert B. Walker, paired with his words of wisdom, motivation, and inspiration.

www.ingramcontent.com/pod-product-compliance
Lightning Source LLC
LaVergne TN
LVHW070155110826
845147LV00002B/412

* 9 7 8 1 9 5 0 4 6 5 1 5 6 *